C000246937

The Search for Thomas Churchyard

An insight into the life and work of the
Woodbridge artist and his family

by Robert Blake

Printed by Technographic, Brightlingsea, Essex

Use of italics to denote titles of paintings
Unless otherwise stated illustrations are watercolours and
attributed to Thomas Churchyard
Provenance where known stated
Size of work where known given in inches (approximate).

Persons featuring in the text are referred to as follows:
T.C. - Thomas Churchyard
Jonathan Churchyard the Younger - father of T.C.
Jonathan the Elder - grandfather of T.C.
E.F.G. - Edward Fitzgerald
B.B. - Bernard Barton
Miss Churchyard or Miss Ellen - the eldest daughter, Ellen
Churchyard
Thomas Churchyard II - Thomas Churchyard, son of T.C.
Charley - Charles Isaac Churchyard, the youngest son of T.C.

Other publications by Robert Blake

Mrs Parsley Remembers: In the Shadow of the Big House, 1990

Woodbridge and Its Environs, 1992

Defection - Why? A Survey by Robert Blake and Sheila Jefferson into why
volunteers volunteer, and also leave charitable agencies, 1993

Melton - A Changing Village, 1994

Contents

My sincere thanks to all those enthusiastic collectors who have allowed me to examine and photograph their Churchyard paintings. It has been their generosity which has made this book possible. The Record Office in Ipswich has shown great patience and given help beyond the call of duty over many years. Jane Sedge and Sally Dummer and the staff of Christchurch Mansion have allowed me to examine their extensive collection of Churchyard paintings and given me much advice and practical help in the preparation of this volume. I have their permission to include a few of their outstanding examples of the Churchyards' work for publication.

My appreciation to Lance Cooper for his expertise and advice on photographic matters.

My good friend John Day, of Eastbourne, has given consistent help and encouragement, for which I am indebted.

Thanks also to Liz Emsley for the typing of the text and to Margaret Hughes for producing the maps and assisting with proof reading.

A special debt is owed to my wife, who has shared my enthusiasm and supported me in this work.

Robert Blake

Overlooking Woodbridge from the Haugh Lane area showing St. Mary's in the centre, oil 6″ x 9″

Roots

It has been my good fortune to have grown up in the part of Suffolk where Thomas Churchyard and his children lived and practised as artists throughout the greater part of the nineteenth century. Our Melton home had examples of their work, as did the homes of many of our friends. My paternal grandmother, Annie Lynda Blake, introduced me at a very early age to the Churchyard family through the good offices of Miss Elsie Redstone, then librarian of the Woodbridge Seckford Library.[1] My grandmother had been a keen amateur artist and, during one momentous visit to Miss Redstone, talked about her painting lessons with the Misses Churchyard, which, to my child's ear, appeared the highest honour. At about this time my grandmother took my brother and me to Christchurch Mansion in Ipswich to look at the Churchyard collection. I recall vividly being told of the location of many of the paintings and how the scenes were still identifiable, even after seventy to one hundred years (an incomprehensible time-scale to a six-year-old). This helped to instil an interest and an empathy in me not only with the Churchyard family but also with the countryside they had loved[2]. Later in my mid-twenties I was given a small album of Churchyard watercolours and, somewhat reluctantly, upon the advice of the late George Arnott[3] decided to split up the collection. I took the eight I considered I liked most, and the remainder were sold over a period of four to five years at the Arnott and Calver Picture Sales in Woodbridge. I was able to frame and keep the eight superb though small watercolours, but sadly these were stolen from my Yorkshire home in the 1980s.

My next encounter with the Churchyards came in 1992 when Lance Cooper and I were preparing our illustrated book "Woodbridge and Its Environs"[4]. My parents had a fine T.C. watercolour of Melton Street and we used this as the back cover for our book. Over the years I had come to admire increasingly not only the great variety of his subjects but also the quality and breadth of his skill and technique.

The life and work of Thomas Churchyard are full of conundrums and mystery. Much of what remains can still - some one hundred and forty years after his death - be found among local enthusiasts and collectors, whose parents and grandparents often knew or, more likely, "knew of" the Churchyard family. By this approach one is immediately confronted with largely unsubstantiated hearsay, gossip, rumour, even legend. The facts themselves are not easy to confirm, as the Churchyards were close-knit in the old Suffolk way and maintained their privacy. Their 'official' careers can be built up and confirmed by diligent research, but what emerges is a group of characters at once shadowy and enigmatic.[5]

Early biographical notes of T.C. tended to be brief and often repeated past inaccuracies. The prevalent view was that this successful nineteenth century Suffolk lawyer enjoyed a largely peaceful life, spending the minimum of time following his

Melton Street

Treeline by river - oil on panel 18" x 26"

professional duties and devoting most of his day as an amateur, self-taught artist to sketching and painting landscapes in and around Woodbridge. His social life was apparently dominated by his friendship with Bernard Barton, the Quaker poet, and with Edward Fitzgerald, a well-to-do intellectual living the life of a dilettante at that time in Boulge. The three friends became known as the Woodbridge Wits, but T.C.' s exact role in the group remains vague. The implication is that the three, often in the company of the Bredfield Rector, George Crabbe, son of George Crabbe the "Poet of Aldeburgh", met for somewhat riotous evenings, usually at the home of Fitzgerald at Boulge Cottage, where they would indulge in "chat, port and toasted cheese, the air being thick with tobacco smoke", and with the occasional barrel of oysters thrown in for luck!

Thomas Churchyard's nine children, particularly his seven unmarried daughters, have been credited with varying but limited degrees of artistic ability; of being imitators of their father's style. Like him, they were all prolific artists, rarely destroying any of their work, a volume of production extending in time to almost a hundred years.[6] Laura's watercolours are usually acknowledged to be closest to those of T.C. The fact that they rarely signed their work inhibits accurate attribution and even adds to the confusion. Only one, Charley (Charles Isaac Churchyard, T.C.'s youngest son) regularly signed, dated and named the venues of his paintings.

In the last thirty years the recognition of the true status of T.C. as an artist in his own right rather than an an imitator of the Norwich School is largely due to the publication of two biographies - Denis Thomas's "Thomas Churchyard of Woodbrldge", and "Painting the Day" by the late Wallace Morfey. Both biographies set out to reveal "the man behind the easel". However, as a contemporary press reviewer noted, each book raises many more questions than it answers. These include - What was the driving force behind his work? Can it be confirmed that he was not commercially motivated in either

Overlooking Woodbridge 10" x 12"

Evening River Scene - oil on panel 12" x 16"

Farm Scene with pigs and man: fine example of T.C.'s work, 10" x 18"

The busy Deben

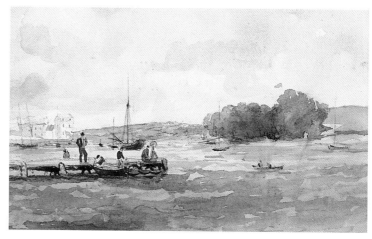

The Tide Mill from Everson's Jetty

his legal practice or his development as an artist? How does his relationship with the Woodbridge Wits fit in? How can we account for the breadth and depth of his style? Why has it taken so long for T.C. to be acknowledged as a leading East Anglian artist whose work is now exhibited in many national collections including the Ashmolean, the Fitzwilliam, the Tate, the V & A and the British Museum, and, nearer to home, Norwich Castle Museum, Christchurch Mansion and the Woodbridge Museum? Since some of the work of his children continues to be attributed to T.C., are there any simple guidelines which can assist the layman to identify T.C.'s own work? How is it that the myths and mysteries concerning T.C. have grown rather than lessened with the passing of time? Does a better understanding of his character and his family assist in the appreciation of his work?

In conjunction with Lance Cooper, I have been collecting photographs of the Churchyard family paintings for many years. These now run into several hundred. With the exception of those pieces in museum ownership, anonymity and confidentiality has been assured to the owners whose Churchyards we have photographed, some of which are illustrated in this volume. We have included a few examples of those artists who knew and worked with the Churchyards and who also painted at the family's favourite venues. Intentionally, not all the illustrations are attributed to Thomas or his children, as on some occasions the actual "authorship" may be in doubt. Characteristics of workmanship and approach are common to all the contemporary "Woodbridge School" of artists. The group included Perry Nursey, John Moore, George Rowe, Henry Bright, Daniel and his son John Brook Hart, Charles Kell, and notably at all times the Churchyard family themselves. It is particularly in Thomas Churchyard's later work - post 1840 - that his confidence, decisive line and indviduality of brushwork is most evident.

Throughout my research I have become increasingly indebted to both Denis Thomas, whose biography "Thomas Churchyard of Woodbridge" confirmed T.C.'s status as a serious artist, and the late Wallace Morfey, whose book "Painting the Day: Thomas Churchyard of Woodbridge" - shows not only his

April Day, Old Melton: oil

Typical T.C. farmyard scene in oil
12" x 11"

extensive knowledge of the period and the contemporary Suffolk scene, but also his unlimited enthusiasm for Thomas Churchyard and his family. This book marked a further step in promoting the "Churchyard cause". It is my loss not to have known Wallace Morfey personally, but I have been fortunate in being able to meet his family and many of his friends, and to examine his papers and notes. In no way does my publication compare with either of its predecessors: I have no hesitation in commending both to the interested reader.

This book gives a brief backdrop of the period; of contemporary life in Woodbridge and its environs, of the Churchyard forbears and, in more detail, of Thomas and his children, his work as an attorney and the accomplishments of the family as artists. My aim is for their sketches and paintings to speak for themselves.

Footnote to Roots

1. T.C.'s daughters, Laura first, then Harriet, had been Librarians at Seckford Library from 1879 to 1926.

2. Wallace Morfey, in a 1981 letter, says "Ninety-five per cent of his work was done within five miles of Woodbridge; identification of the location, especially if buildings or the Deben are included is often still possible despite the long passage of time, which can be in excess of 150 years. "

3. George Arnott was senior partner at the family firm of Arnott and Calver, Woodbridge estate agents and auctioneers in Church Street. He was a well-known art connoisseur and local historian, whose published books include 'Suffolk Estuary', 'Alde Estuary', 'Orwell Estuary', and 'The Place Names of the Deben Valley Parishes'.

4. Lance Cooper - a long-established professional photographer of Woodbridge - who collaborated with me in preparing for publication "Woodbridge and its Environs" (1992), an illustrated book arising from our collection of old photographs, paintings and memorabilia.

5. Martin Davies, the social psychologist and keen Churchyard collector, perceptively says "The figures in their paintings are usually shadowy, rarely defined and elusive, like themselves".

6. Early examples of T.C.'s work date from 1820, and the last works of Harriet and Charley Churchyard are post 1914-18 War.

Right: Farm Scene
8″ x 12″
Far right: At Walberswick
4″ x 5¹/₂″
Below: 'At Melton'
2¹/₂″ x 5″

An angler on the banks of the Deben with St Mary's Church beyond - oil on canvas 19$\frac{1}{2}$" x 18"

Local boy made good

The Churchyard family tree can be traced, like my own, back to its mid-sixteenth century Suffolk yeoman roots. Over some two centuries the Churchyards migrated from North Suffolk to the Framlingham and Woodbridge region. It was Jonathan, the enterprising son of Charles and Mary Churchyard, farmers of Charsfield,[1] who broke out of the poverty trap by setting up a small butchery business in Melton, following his marriage to Hannah Waspe of Ufford in 1768. He quickly rose in wealth and influence above his artisan siblings in Charsfield, Wickham Market, Ufford and Woodbridge. The location of his Melton Street shop was an important contributory factor, standing as it did at an increasingly important business and route centre, a mile north of Woodbridge, which was the area's largest market town and inland port.

The great London Road from Southtown (Yarmouth) passed by Jonathan's shop on its way to the metropolis; added to this, roads from the rich highlands of central Suffolk came to Melton. The main routes from the coastal light-lands[2] converged on Wilford Bridge, the lowest bridging point of the Deben, less than half a mile from his butcher's shop. Another asset was its acre or so of land (formerly the village pyghtle), with slaughterhouse and tannery[3] which were to play a significant role in increasing the family's wealth over the next sixty years.

Jonathan's rising status and authority within the community was confirmed when he became People's Warden at St Andrew's Church, Melton, Assessor of the Poor Rate and Overseer of the Poor, together with his appointment as purveyor of meat to Melton's House of Industry (Poorhouse)[4].

His business as a cattle dealer and drover had also been expanding over the years. From 1784 he drove pigs to Smithfield Market, some 78 miles from Melton, on a regular

Wilford Bridge from Mt Pleasant (site of Melton Grange)
8" x 12"

Early T.C. study from Wilford Hollows overlooking Wilford Bridge

The Churchyard Family

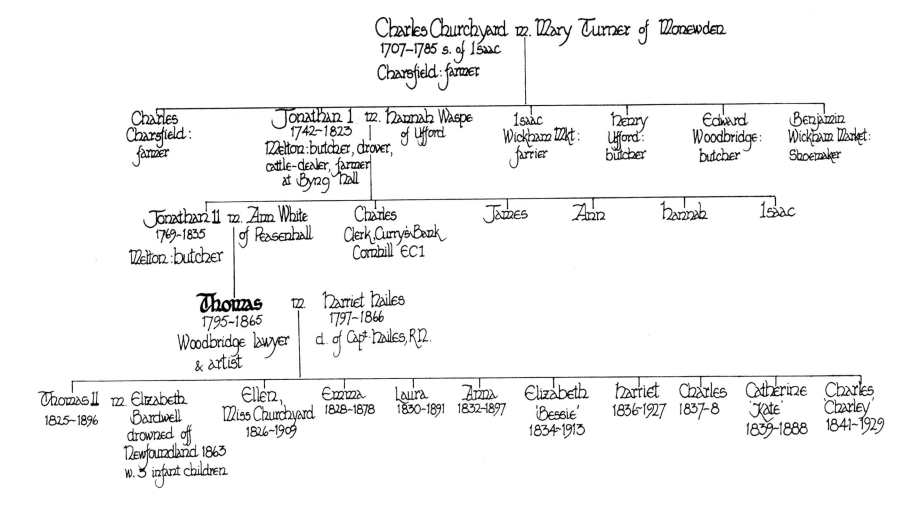

Charles Churchyard m. Mary Turner of Monewden
1707–1785 s. of Isaac
Charsfield: farmer

Charles
Charsfield:
farmer

Jonathan 1 m. Hannah Waspe
1742–1823   of Ufford
Melton: butcher, drover,
cattle-dealer, farmer
at Byng Hall

Isaac
Wickham Mkt:
farrier

Henry
Ufford:
butcher

Edward
Woodbridge:
butcher

Benjamin
Wickham Market:
Shoemaker

Jonathan 11 m. Ann White
1769–1835   of Peasenhall
Melton: butcher

Charles
Clerk, Curry's Bank
Cornhill EC1

James   Ann   Hannah   Isaac

Thomas   m.   Harriet Hailes
1795–1865   1797–1866
Woodbridge lawyer   d. of Capt. Hailes, R.N.
& artist

Thomas 11   m. Elizabeth
1825–1896   Bardwell
                drowned off
                Newfoundland 1863
                w. 5 infant children

Ellen,
Miss Churchyard
1826–1909

Emma
1828–1878

Laura
1830–1891

Anna
1832–1897

Elizabeth
'Bessie'
1834–1913

Harriet
1836–1927

Charles
1837–8

Catherine
'Kate'
1839–1888

Charles
'Charley'
1841–1929

Unloading grain from barge at New Quay 8" x 10"

Full Sail on the Deben

fortnightly basis[5]. In 1792 he took his eldest son Jonathan (the Younger) into partnership, and they now included sheep on the droves, enlarging the catchment area to Snape. In addition he also "attended" the Romford market on a regular basis. The problems, particularly of communication, adverse weather conditions, possible loss of cattle, obtaining and maintaining adequate "layering"[6] venues en route, and the complications of having a number of different herds on the road at the same time, all necessitated efficient organisation. If a crisis should arise it could have had daunting financial consequences. However, the profits when all the factors went well were considerable, more than compensating for the risks involved.

Charles, the second son, left Melton to seek his fortune in London as a clerk at about the same time that Jonathan the Younger was taken into partnership with their father. Both brothers, through their endeavours, rose steadily in their respective careers over the next few years. Jonathan the Younger, as we have seen, took over the Melton butchery business, while Charles eventually became Chief Clerk to Currie's, the London bankers. Jonathan the Elder's retirement in 1804 allowed him to concentrate on farming with the assistance of James and Isaac, his younger sons, first at Blocks Barn on the outskirts of Melton, then a holding of some sixty acres, which he owned. Byng Hall, with its 112 acres rented from Lord Rendlesham, became his residence after he left the butcher's shop, and was regarded by the Churchyards as their "family seat". Finally, Jonathan the Elder added Florey's Farm, Clopton, to his estate by direct purchase in the same year, 1804.

Jonathan the Younger's marriage to Anne, daughter of Thomas White, "a substantial grocer, draper and entrepreneur"[8] of Peasenhall, brought not only money to the union but also added considerable social consequence to the family. The

Parkland study

Woodland scene 5" x 4³/4"

Study of Silver Birches - oil on canvas 10" x 8"

Whites had wide-ranging business interests from an extended network, which included shop-keeping, farming and auctioneering and could claim kinship from a complex family tree with the leading county families. Thomas, an only child, was born in 1798, and as the only son and grandson it was in his future that the family vested great expectations. As in many self-made and 'upwardly mobile' families, Thomas was destined to have materially the best they could provide without apparent restraint. The cultivation of thrift was not part of hls upbringing: throughout his life he failed to comprehend the need for its application.

It can be argued that Thomas's intelligence and pleasing personality, combined with a sound education enabled him to rise from the artisan to the professional class, a step which in the early nineteenth century had a far greater significance than in today's world. While his parents provided the best education

Bridge reflection on the upper Deben
4" x 3"

they could give him as a boarder at Dedham, the leading East Suffolk grammar school of the day, he was nevertheless set on a course which would isolate him from his peers in Melton: "He was destined to be educated beyond his class." A part of him, nevertheless, was always firmly anchored to his Churchyard family and forbears. The years from 1808 to 1816 spent in transit from his Melton environs to the more rarefied life of Dedham and back again were to set the seal on his

philosophy of life and his future career. Academically he benefited from Dedham, but life there must have been far removed from that of his Melton roots, with his family's flourishing and expanding "rough and tumble" business interests, with which his father and grandfather were so actively concerned. It would mean that from an early age Thomas had a foot in both camps - that of the more sophisticated professional class encountered at Dedham, and

Earliest known example of T.C.'s work, signed and dated 1819

that of his rustic Melton neighbours together with members of his immediate and extended family. He would learn early that different behavioural patterns must be applied immediately and often with subtlety if he was to maintain hls own personal identity and integrity. He had no siblings with whom to compete or even to compare his development. The trait of keeping his own counsel, established early, can be traced throughout his life. At times he was over-zealous in maintaining confidentiality, and his friends (and in all probability his family) found him somewhat secretive. Unpleasant realities, particularly those concerning finance, were often evaded, while procrastination became a characteristic of his later years. His parents, while naturally proud of their son's progress, and with his and their future in mind, would have tended to protect and isolate him still further. It is interesting to speculate as to the significance of the loneliness, engendered during childhood, which was to influence many aspects of T.C.'s adult behaviour. His expectations during his early years were bright and full of promise. From Dedham Grammar School Thomas was articled to a Halesworth firm of solicitors before graduating in 1822, with the title of Attorney, and with it the right to feel himself almost a "gentleman". Surprisingly, perhaps, he set up as a Woodbridge attorney, thus fulfilling one old Suffolk maxim "Always progress beyond your roots" and breaking another "Never try to better yourself in your own backyard".

Footnote to Local boy made good

1. The setting for Ronald Blyth's famous "Akenfleld", published in 1969.

2. Lightlands - areas of coastal sandy soil used predominantly for sheep rearing in the nineteenth century.

3. By coincidence I own much of the property adjacent to the Churchyard holding and the old deeds I hold clearly show the extent of Jonathan's property.

4. Site of St Audrey's Hospital, Melton, now (1997) redundant and being developed for residential use.

5. "Jonathan Churchyard, Drover and Salesman in Melton near Woodbridge in Suffolk gives Notice that He intends drawing in Pigs for London fortnightly." Advertisement from the Ipswich Journal, September 1784.

6. Layering - renting secure and enclosed land suitable for resting the animals overnight while travelling to market.

7. Mason, Currie, James and Yellaby, Bankers, 29 Cornhill, London.

8. My great great great grandfather being Thomas Girling, a kinsman of the Peasenhall Whites. His Commonplace Book is much quoted by Wallace Morfey in his book "Painting the Day".

'Thoughts of Summer'
Believed to be copy of 17th century Dutch painting
in his possesion at some time. Provenance
purchased at the 1927 sale.

His life was beset with contradictions

Mrs Harriet Churchyard 1825

There are contradictions, mysteries and unanswered questions surrounding Thomas Churchyard and his life. Many of the accepted aspects of his work are open to speculation and after even cursory research and some "teasing out" can be challenged if not completely over-ruled. Examination of several hundred examples of his work over the last two to three years has been of incomparable benefit; of these we have photographed over five hundred examples. One has to say that in some ways the picture is now less clear than before we began this task. I had certain preconceived ideas which I now appreciate are open to challenge and reconsideration. It was my early understanding, for instance, that T.C. did not paint portraits, but a few attributed to him have been examined, and without doubt the fine oil of his young daughter Ellen (Miss Churchyard), who was probably sixteen to seventeen years of age at the time, is his work. The much earlier watercolour portrait of 'Mrs Harriet Churchyard', signed and dated 1825 at the time of their marriage, and that of A. Redgrave, both show more than competence. Buildings and figures are quoted by some authorities as not being his forte. This premise must be open to question. Denis Thomas's biography 'Thomas Churchyard of Woodbridge', published 1966, is illustrated with a very strong painting of Ely, while we have photographed many fine, detailed sketches and watercolours which concentrate on architectural merits rather than the general landscape. Figures are not always in the distance, walking away from the easel, and certainly not shadowy, but given a significantly prominent position in the scene. I believe we can disregard the legend (suggested by George Arnott and others) that Charley was responsible for adding the figures, either at the time of composition or later. Time and again, however, one finds the same figures - often two ladies or a lady and a child walking away into the background, or the one-legged figure (apparently a veteran of the Napoleonic wars who lived in the Woodbridge area). We also have the cart, either being driven into the distance or stationary, placed strategically in the landscape. These techniques often give a better perspective and realism to a painting.

Wallace Morfey's biography cites an early T.C. painting dated (which in itself is unusual)[1] and entitled Thomas Churchyard 1820", the original now located in South Africa. Wallace Morfey details the watercolour as having St Mary's and the Abbey in the background with reapers cutting corn with their sickles, binding the sheaves and setting up stooks in the foreground. He makes a point of the way T.C. painted, facing the early sun and how he boldly scored the paper with a circle and a radius. Recently we examined and photographed what I believe to be a near replica of the work referred to by Wallace Morfey which has been in the Woodbridge area since the 1930s and which the owner believed to be the work of George Rowe[2] dating from the mid-1820s. I suggest two possible explanations. Either the two

Jetty Lane, now the Avenue and Kingston field

'After Crome' 8" x 12"

Early watercolour circa 1820's attributed at different times to both T.C. and George Rowe. Many oils and watercolours of this subject exist - some have been engraved and published

Above: Fine portrait of Miss Churchyard circa 1840 - inscribed Ellen
Left: Anna 'en plein air' Drawing by papa 7" x 4"

Christmas holly sprig: signed and dated

Above: Celebrations at Woodbridge Abbey in gouache, signed T.C. and dated 1831.
Below: Woods' Nursery - Notcutt's from 1897

Pencil sketch - Boat Inn 3" x 4"

Boat Inn 6" x 8" (differnt date from pencil sketch)

nearly identical pieces were part of a learning process whereby a self-taught amateur artist without direction of a mentor faithfully copied work until he had mastered, to his own satisfaction, technique and style; or the venue used by the artist (in this case T.C.) was visited time and again by him, his artist friends and his children, resulting in many versions of the same scene. In support of this theory we know that T.C. (like his daughters) was a good copyist, and one of the delights he had in purchasing paintings by recognised masters (particularly Gainsborough, Crome, Morland and later Constable) was in order not only to study their work in his own home but also to copy their paintings for his own personal satisfaction and in order to develop his own technique.   In the case of a few

Constable attributions it has been claimed that some are in fact T.C.'s renderings! My own feeling is that T.C. was a sociable person who enjoyed sketching and painting in company with his friends and later with his daughters, and this could explain why, a hundred to a hundred and fifty years after the original painting, we find what appear to be faithful copies. Since the Renaissance copying has had an honourable place in what may now be termed the 'learning curve' of apprentice artists. In the Churchyard family the mentor was often otherwise engaged in the Courts or on 'the picture chase' while his pupils practised. We can safely assume that copying was integral to their art education.

Wickham Market square, signed and dated 1837 on back (N.B. also typical example of T.C. ' Holly Study', which he used on Christmas cards sent to close friends and family)

After John Cromes 'The Windmill'

'Sunset' - bold ,strong work after Turner 8" x 10"

Oil of Lime Kiln Quay: has been attributed both to T.C. and more recently to George Rowe. 8″ x 10″   There are several oils and watercolours where attribution to either artist is open to question.

From Wilford Hollows or Gallows Hill

Farm Scene 4" x 8"

Melton woods, oil on panel 3¹/₂" x 4¹/₂"

Copy of a Morland

Footnotes to His life was beset with contradictions

1. Few of his paintings are either signed or dated, but when they are there probably is a significant reason. For example, his collection of six pen-and-ink sketches signed and dated 1819 may have recorded a series of memorable days spent touring and sketching through Norfolk and Suffolk; or perhapscarefully crafted copies of engravings which he completed at the end of this time articled at Halesworth.

The fine and detailed watercolour portrait of 'Mrs Harriet Churchyard', dated 1825, the year of their marriage.

The view of Wickham Market Square signed and dated 1837 could possibly be an oblique reference to members of his family who lived and traded there. Perhaps he combined a professional visit~ with a family visit. Certainly it would appear that the simple pen-and-ink sketch would not warrant special treatment.

The fact that he signed and dated his personal Christmas cards sent to his friends speaks for itself.

2. George James Rowe, 1804-1883 (on occasions his signature reads James George Rowe), landscape artist whose father, a retired naval surgeon, lived in Well Street (now Seckford Street), Woodbridge. George Rowe was a lifelong friend of T.C. In 1832 they left Woodbridge together in an abortive attempt to establish themselves as professional landscape artists. In recent years George Rowe's artistic status has greatly improved.

The Woodbridge Scene

Thomas Churchyard's social life was dominated during the crucial years[1] of the 1840s by his association with the 'chief Woodbridge Wits', but we do get other glimpses, particularly earlier, that help build up our wider understanding of the type of person he really was. George James Rowe not only accompanied him to London in 1832 on their abortive attempt to become professional landscape artists but was always a friend of the family. Henry Bright[2], another nineteenth century Woodbridge artist, shares many of the characteristics of T.C.'s 'natural landscape' style. Daniel Hart, the wealthy Woodbridge maltster and keen amateur artist, was another lifelong friend

Woodbridge from Fen Meadow: Charles Kell. St. John's Church spire dates this to post 1846

Brightwell Church - After Constable 14" x 11"
Painted at the same location as John Constable but some twenty years later (see p.97).

The Old Lucy at Woodbridge Quay

who shared the company of T.C. on his painting forays. T.C. would have known Perry Nursey[3], another prolific and skilled Woodbridge landscape artist, who lived at The Grove, Little Bealings, less than four miles from Woodbridge. The choice of painting venues as well as general style are further confirmation of T.C.'s "working relationships" with contemporary local artists. Many paintings by George Moore and Charles Kell can be seen to be so close to the work of T.C. that they have been (and still are) often incorrectly attributed to him. From a very early age his children accompanied him on painting expeditions, their work throughout their lives demonstrating his influence.

Moot Hall Aldeburgh: from collection of the late Bryan Hall and originally purchased from the 1927 Churchyard sale   6″x 7³/₄″

Dunwich oil

Dunwich watercolour

The controversy concerning T.C.'s relationship with John Constable persists. Without doubt T.C. admired, respected and imitated the painter's style. Major Hart always maintained that Daniel Hart, his grandfather, together with T.C. 'hob-nobbed' and went sketching with Constable when the latter stayed in Woodbridge. We know that Constable did in fact stay in the district on several occasions. I have seen a fine, large (16 x 14 inches vertical) T.C. watercolour of Brightwell Church painted from exactly the same position as that chosen by Constable in his 1816 oil. One could guess by the changed landscape that the Churchyard painting could be some ten to twenty years later, i.e. circa 1830. It is known that Constable came to Woodbridge in 1830 to re-purchase his oil of Helmingham Dell from the Pulham Estate in order to prevent it being sold too cheaply in a Woodbridge auction. The theory that on his later visit Constable spent some time painting in the area, possibly accompanied by T.C. and maybe Daniel Hart and Perry Nursey,

is given some credence by the firmly held local legend that they did in fact spend a day at Brightwell, some four miles from Woodbridge. If T.C. had not known Constable or his painting of Brightwell Church, why should he choose precisely the same location for his own painting?

Constable's magnificent 1820 portrait of Mrs Pulham would certainly have involved several sittings in Woodbridge and therefore more than one visit by the artist. It is likely that he would have spent some time socialising, and at this time T.C. was either coming to the end of his articles at Halesworth, or had in fact already returned to live with his parents at Melton. In either event the friendly and extrovert personality of T.C. would make it likely that they would have become acquainted. Certainly T.C.'s style, particularly during his early formative years (1820-1840) was very close to that of Constable. Throughout his life T.C. held Constable in very high regard and at times owned several of his paintings.

From Highgate HIll towards St Pauls, thought to be after Constable   4" x 5 1/2"

Tree Study

The most important evidence for a close relationship between the two is surely the visit of Constable's son to Woodbridge and to Churchyard soon after the death of Constable in 1837. Immediately after this visit T.C. wrote a full account of the circumstances of John Constable's death (as related by his son) - in itself an unusual procedure for T.C. to take (i.e. to record an event in such a way). The document written in T.C.'s hand in 1837 was not discovered until 1927, following the death of the last surviving Churchyard daughter, Harriet.

Churchyard's love for the variety of country life is evident in his paintings. He relished spending days with his friends shooting game in the Woodbridge area. From many of his paintings one can see that he enjoyed time passed both on and close to the Deben. Family holidays were spent usually at Aldeburgh, Dunwich or Felixstowe, but sometimes in southern England, and on one occasion in 1853 they travelled as far afield as Weston-Super-Mare. All are found recorded in his paintings. It remains, however, difficult to place his work with accuracy into the correct time scale, as many of his sketches and paintings appear rough and undated. There are paintings executed in or around London, which could date from his visits to his uncle, the Cornhill banker's clerk, to his Hailes in-laws at Covent Garden, or from the months when he and George Rowe were attempting to establish themselves as professional artists. A further complication is that after this early period he continued to make many trips to the metropolis, sketching and painting watercolours during his time away from Woodbridge.

Early work influenced by J. Crome, George Frost and Gainsborough. Oil on panel 22¹/₄" x 27"

Aldeburgh Church by Laura 4″ x 6″

Slaughden, Aldeburgh by Laura

Melton Old Church pre 1868 when building was much reduced in size, attributed to T.C. or Laura.

The association with Edward Fitzgerald, Bernard Barton and George Crabbe, the so-called Woodbridge wits[4], presents to us now the most compelling portrait of what T.C., the person was like in middle life. The role of Edward Fitzgerald is crucial to any interpretation of T.C.'s character and understanding of his developing financial crises, which became manifest to his family during the last twenty years of his life, even if not to T.C. himself. E.F.G. was the catalyst. His wealth, his position as gentry, his status as a Cambridge graduate, an intellectual and above all their shared passion for collecting paintings account for the attraction between them in the early 1840s. T.C. may have seen this hand of friendship as a compliment, particularly to a working country attorney, whose family (many still living in and around Woodbridge) came from humble artisan stock. T.C. could well have come to E.F.G.'s eye long before they became friends. T.C. was notable among his contemporary Woodbridgeans in that he was not afraid to be his own man, in his personal as well as his professional life. His work as a lawyer brought him into the public arena where his growing reputation as the "Poacher's Lawyer" and champion of the poor meant that confrontation with the landed gentry throughout Suffolk and beyond could not have gone unnoticed. While winning enthusiastic comment in country ale houses, his adversaries in their farmhouses, halls and mansions, must have viewed him with reservation and concern.

T.C.'s personal life was full of colour, providing material for gossip. His association with the Hailes family and subsequent marriage to the heavily pregnant Harriet must have been much talked about by all classes in the Woodbridge area of 1825. From this distance of time we can appreciate some of the attraction of the extrovert Halles family for him. In contrast to his own life, theirs was very colourful both before and after they came to live in Melton some ten years prior to his marriage. Wallace Morfey clearly but gently sets the scene for the Hailes family when he writes "All a little bit more elevated within the family than in the official world"[5]. The naval career

Thomas Churchyard's sketch of Melton Spring engraved by J. Hawksworth, Published in 1834

Satirical sketch of shooting party, pen and ink, probably the work of Miss Churchyard, Kate or Harriet

View of St Mary's from Ipswich Road with stage coach approaching and the familiar elongated figure in the right hand foreground. 7" x 6"

Lions' Den, Bromeswell 6" x 8"

of his future father-in-law, "Captain"[6] George Hailes, although not devoid of travel and action in the early years from its commencement in 1776, certainly "did not turn out to be a brilliant one" according to Wallace Morfey. He saw action in the West Indies but within six to eight years was shore-based and so he remained for the remainder of his career until his retirement in 1818. The marriage of George Hailes to Susan Harris, the eighteen-year-old daughter from a wealthy Essex

Gypsy encampment at Wilford Hollows from a T.C. watercolour, engraved by Hawksworth, published in the Sudbury Pocket Book 1834 1" x 2"

'The Valley of Fern' T.C. drawing, engraved by Hawksworth and published 1834 in the Sudbury Pocket Book 1" x 2"

Sailors rowing out from shore, oil on canvas 8" x 11"

farming family, was not without incident. Their first son had already been born outside wedlock, being followed over the subsequent twelve years of marriage by four more sons and five daughters. However, the Hailes family and Thomas

Churchyard had one significant thing in common: they were all well educated and had risen into the professional world.

One factor that would have caused the Hailes family to be even more 'in the public eye' was the eventual separation of 'the

Seckford Street - late nineteenth century study by Charley Churchyard, (close to the residence of the 'Little White Mice' at the old schoolmasters home, 3 Seckford Street) 8" x 6"

Farm at Melton with stacked corn and poppies in foreground - a favourite format found in many paintings of T.C.

Farm house and buildings, oil 9″ x 10″

'The Beeches', Melton: a modern photograph. The Churchyards lived here 1833 - 43

View of Deben at Waldringfield 6" x 4"

Captain' and his wife from 1820, when she left him in Melton and took up residence with a married daughter at St Clement's Parish in Ipswich. To do this would not have been common one hundred and fifty years ago, nor was it socially acceptable and it would certainly not have passed unnoticed.

The Ipswich Journal in January 1825 boldly announced the marriage of "Thomas Churchyard, solicitor of Woodbridge, to Harriet Hailes". It is difficult to imagine that the marriage would have added to his status as an attorney or his standing in the staid local community. The birth of their son (Thomas II) two months later in Woodbridge was a clear statement of T.C.'s disregard for local sensitivities - there was for him to be no secret wedding and subsequent birth, with the subtle later introduction of mother and child without the details and dates which were often glossed over in the nineteenth century world. (The Churchyard family bible did omit to give the date of the marriage between Thomas and Harriet.) T.C. and his new wife set up home at 29 Well Street (now 29 Seckford Street), and in rapid succession four further children were born until,

***Self portrait in middle age
by Thomas Churchyard***

dramatically, in 1832, T.C. decided to sell up[7], and leave Woodbridge to set himself up in London as a professional artist. Speculation is open as to the domestic arrangements made for Harriet and their young family, but in all probability they went to live with Thomas's mother, now widowed, who had some wealth and property in Melton.

The London venture was a disaster. Neither he nor George Rowe could establish themselves as professional artists. The current economy alone was against them. With the industrial and agricultural slump, social and economic unrest, the art market in disarray, the time was not favourable to set out on this career, and T.C. returned to Woodbridge within eight months to his old profession as an attorney. For the next ten years the family lived at the Beeches, Melton.

Melton village today bears little resemblance to that of some one hundred and fifty years ago. Although less than a mile from Woodbridge, it was still virtually self-sufficient, with all the basic trades and services located in the main street. Throughout these years many of T.C.'s most impressive landscapes, particularly those of the Deben, showing Wilford Bridge, Melton Quay, and the Docks, were executed. His sketches and watercolours of Melton Spring, Wilford Hollows, and the 'Valley of Fern' (Appendix 1) which Hawksworth engraved for publication in the 'Sudbury Pocket Books' all date from the 1830s.

Woodbridge was the important cynosure of their lives. It was the largest and most thriving market town in the area, some eight miles north of Ipswich on the main coaching route from London to Southtown (Great Yarmouth). It was the largest port on the Deben, and as such the market town had grown immensely during the early years of the nineteenth century. This can be verified by the virtual doubling of the customs collected between 1834 (£2,263) and 1840 (£4,315). New warehouses, quays, and improved docks, all enhanced the viability of Woodbridge port.

Satirical sketch by Ellen dated 1852, possibly depicting the Woodbridge Wits. Bernard Barton on left, Charley next to him, Edward Fitzgerald in centre and T.C. on right.

Marston House, Cumberland Street.
Home of the Churchyards 1843 - 1853

Then as now the Thoroughfare, the central arterial street, dominated the town. The best shops were situated there; Church Street (formerly Stone Street) led from the Cross Corner to the Market Hill with its impressive Dutch gabled Shire Hall. St Mary's Church was nearby, and from 1843 St John's Church, ensuring that the town lived up to the claim in White's 1844 Suffolk Directory that it had "several handsome public buildings".

Market Day in Churchyard's time was the liveliest of the week. We can only imagine the hustle and bustle (if not chaos) which would begin early in the day with the drovers bringing cattle, pigs, geese, not to mention poultry, and other livestock, and produce for sale. The Petty Sessions sitting in the upper part of the Shire Hall also offered excitement for some. It was certainly during these formative years that T.C.'s reputation as an attorney was established and, like his family his social life grew and matured. He was a familiar Woodbridge figure, and although small in stature, a "petit person", as E.F.G. on occasions commented ('my little friend'), he moved quickly, "rushing hither and thither", always attracted by some novelty or excitement[8]. His friendship with Bernard Barton, the Quaker poet, was well established by 1839, and this is confirmed by the special lines composed to commemorate his 41st birthday, spent at the Beeches (see Appendix 2). In many ways, Bernard Barton can be seen as the "go-between" from E.F.G. to T.C. As already noted, T.C. was no correspondent and this is continually lamented in the letters of B.B. and E.F.G. Messages are relayed backwards and forwards for "Mr Churchyard" or on other occasions "our legal friend" or "our artist" and this aversion to committing himself to paper can partly be explained by T.C.'s legal training, recognising how significant written evidence can be and how easily it can be misconstrued or taken out of context. His life was so full that lack of time alone made writing difficult if not impossible, certainly upon

Harvest Scene

the scale indulged in by B.B. and E.F.G., one of whose chief interests letter-writing was.

The mutual interests between the three men, who, in conjunction with the Reverend George Crabbe, made up,

according to E.F.G.'s dictum, the chief Woodbridge Wits, can be understood. They all loved the local Suffolk countryside around Woodbridge; we can imagine T.C. and E.F.G. sailing up and down the Deben, painting and drawing. 'Within six miles

Late T.C. watercolour 'Sunset over the Deben'   3¹/₂" x 5"

Woodland scene with tree shadows Oil on panel 8¹/₂″ x 12¹/₂″

of Woodbridge no place was untouched by Churchyard's brush', wrote E.F.G., who was a keen artist at times himself and reasonably competent, both sketching and working in watercolours. Bernard Barton composed many poems enthusing over the charms and qualities of country life:

Thou Deben art dear to me;
Thou hast thy own befitting charms
Of quiet heath and fertile farms,
With here and there a copse to fling
Its welcome shade, where wild birds sing;
Thy meads for flocks and herds to graze;
The quays and docks where seamen raise
Their anchor and unfurl their sail
To woo and win the favouring gale.
And above all, for me the host
Endearing memories of the Past.

Both B,B, and T,C. had a special affection for 'The Valley of Fern', one of a number of narrow and deep valleys leading down to the Deben at Woodbridge. Many T.C. paintings record 'The Valley of Fern' from different vantage points, and Hawksworth etched perhaps his most famous, which was published in the Sudbury Pocket Book of 1835. Barton's poem enthusing over this valley is especially poignant since most of this area in recent years has been built over.

The Valley of Fern

Part I

There is a lone valley, few charms can it number,
Compared with the lovely glens north of the Tweed;
No mountains enclose it where morning mists slumber,
And it never has echoed the shepherd's soft reed.
No streamlet of crystal, its rocky banks laving,
Flows through it, delighting the ear and the eye;
On its sides no proud forests, their foliage waving,
Meet the gales of the autumn or the summer wind's sigh;
Yet by me it is prized, and full dearly I love it,
And oft my Steps thither I pensively turn;
It has silence within, heaven's proud arch above it,
And my fancy has named it the Valley of Fern.

Part II

Thou art changed, lovely spot! and no more thou displayest,
To the eye of thy votary, that negligent grace,
Which, in moments the saddest, the tenderest, the gayest,
Allured him so oft thy recesses to trace.
The hand of the spoiler has fallen upon thee,
And marr'd the wild beauties that deck thee before;
And the charms, which a poet's warm praises had won thee,
Exist but in memory, and bless thee no more.
The green, palmy fern, which the softest and mildest
Of summer's light breezes could ruffle, - is fled;
And the bright-blossom'd ling, which spread o'er thee her wildest
And wantonest hues, - is uprooted and dead.

Bernard Barton, c. 1817.

Photograph of T.C. and Laura circa 1860

of Bredfield, eldest son of George Crabbe, the eighteenth century Aldeburgh poet was an ebullient personality all his life, an asset in company. Their common interests were intellectual. They enjoyed the evenings of animated conversation, entertaining each other in their respective homes. They were able to talk freely and in confidence, relishing especially, when at Boulge Cottage the meals provided by Mrs Faier, E.F.G.'s faithful housekeeper who sent from the kitchen "course after course" of well prepared dishes as the wits continued their animated discussions, "oiled by quality wines-and porter", "the air thick with clouds of tobacco smoke". We can surmise the topics would range from politics to pictures, from figures of national and local interest to events in the art world.

The thread that runs through all the correspondence between E.F.G. and B.B., indeed through all T.C.'s life, marks him as an avid connoisseur and collector of paintings. His credentials were well established by the time of his 1832 auction. Over the following years the habit of buying, exchanging "wheeling, dealing and bartering" paintings, particularly those of the Norwich School, had become an essential feature of his everyday life. The time and energy spent in chasing, examining and eventually purchasing, whether in public auction both locally and in town or through dealers and "runners", must have been enormous and this initially was clearly what attracted E.F.G. and, to a lesser extent B.B., to Churchyard. They were, like him, keen collectors. All three were familiar with the contemporary intricacies of the London and provincial auction rooms and those personalities and characters who most frequented them and made their livings from assisting in the exchange of works of art.

When E.F.G. purchased paintings he certainly respected and increasingly relied upon T.C.'s judgement: "My new painting (a Constable) is admired and is reckoned quite genuine by our great judge, Mr. Churchyard." This letter, from E.F.G. to B.B., dated 1843, was in the early days of E.F.G.'s growing friendship with T.C., and as the years passed he came to respect his counsel beyond his knowledge of paintings.

They each contributed different qualities to the circle. E.F.G. had the ease of manner resulting from an upper class life and outlook. B.B., of humble Quaker stock, was a prolific poet and correspondent but not, perhaps, as puritanical as one might expect, enjoying with the others the good things of life. T.C. was an established country lawyer and an artist of growing merit with a large family. The Reverend George Crabbe, Rector

Vecta: signed and dated by Ellen, May '58.   *Spring flowers: Ellen Churchyard (attrib) 10" x 8".*

Study of Pansies, masculine in feeling.
Botanical paintings were not Charley's forte
so we conclude this to be the work of T.C.

These pen and ink works were from T.C.'s famous courtroom sketches

The effect on T.C.'s career and social life of his growing collecting addiction can only be guessed at. From the correspondence of E.F.G. and B.B. it is clear that all three appreciated and enjoyed the "chase" of searching out and often purchasing paintings. But for T.C. there was the additional lure of being able to examine in his own home the technique of other recognised and established artists.

For many years he was seen as an imitator, rather than as an initiator. The compulsion to purchase pictures over the last twenty-five years of life, despite his developing financial problems, went on unabated. In fact, his buying increased, and perhaps became a way of escape from the less pleasant aspects of his life. He sold and passed on paintings, often very quickly, as his enthusiasm waned or as other paintings and artists presented themselves, or, less likely, as financial prudence prevailed. We have no accounts as to the sums involved, except for the year 1843, but at a modest estimate he spent several thousand pounds during this period, which would represent a

Memorandum
June 26th 1864

Sold to Mr. B. Moulton
a Picture by Old Crome
Back of the New Mills
Norwich   £ 63

Recd in payment as
under
Picture by Constable   20
Do. by T. Churchyard   8
Do. by Old Crome Norwich
Cathedral   20
Cash to balance   15
                                £ 63

Thos. Churchyard

Benj Moulton
3

June 20th 1865

Mem.

This day deposited
with Mr. Robt Millen
two pictures by Crome
(that is to say) one of
Boat builders yard
Norwich "the other"
an upright picture of
buildings at Norwich
to secure the sum of
£80 and interest
at £8 per cent -
to be redeemed at any time
on payment of principal
money and Interest
Thos Churchyard

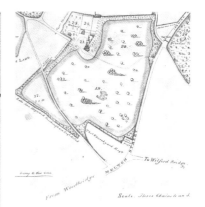

Taken from conveyancing document dated December 1848 and clearly confirming that at this date T.C. owned a large block of property adjacent to Melton Street.

Far left: Document dated some fourteen months before his death
Left: Document writen only nine months before T.C.s death confirming his increasingly precarious finances

fraction of today's value. What we are unable to calculate is what he received in return from the sales. Did he make money from picture dealing? The character of T.C. is strongly indicative that he did not. He was not a cautious person; no calculating salesman waiting for the right customer and being prepared to enter into protracted negotiations. Clearly he did not spend time or care in promoting the sales of paintings from his collection. B.B.s assessment of T.C.'s artistic abilities also confirm his character: "Churchyard will dash you off slight and careless sketches by the dozen or score, but as for touching, retouching or finishing, that is quite another affair." He certainly made no attempt to promote himself as a serious artist, rarely exhibiting[9], and there is no record of his ever accepting commissions or selling his work. Over the years we have examined a large number of T.C.'s paintings in completely representational style. In contrast however, some of the work executed during the last ten - twenty years of his life reveal his own distinctive impressionistic mode.

Windmill: oil 5" x 8"

Throughout his life he showed no appreciation of the value of money - even when he was married with a large family when he ought to have known the necessity of prudence, there are few indications of financial restraint. The Churchyards lived well, and from 1843, when they moved to Marston House, Woodbridge, considered to be one of the finest town houses, they lived in some style. Marston House doubled as an office for T.C., the lawyer, and a home for his wife and by then nine children (eight of whom were to remain unmarried and live with their father until his death in 1865). T.C. normally employed two clerks at Marston House in addition to the resident domestic staff of at least three which included Miss Bird, their long term governess. This would have been a drain on any professional person and the indications are that following the death of his mother in 1843, he had to capitalise continually on the funds and properties he had inherited. Times continued to be unfavourable, the national economy being depressed throughout these years.

We know that he spent time "each and every day"[10] sketching and painting, and this was true for all his children. The salient question is how profitable was his professional career? Being acknowledged as the "Poacher's Lawyer" was not promising. These were the days before the provision of Legal Aid, when representing the underclass could rarely have been financially rewarding. We read of instances where, in court and publicly, T.C. waived his clients' costs - how often did this occur unofficially? With his acknowledged social conscience, did T.C. make adequate professional charges-to his poorer clients? Was he often, or, at least on occasion, paid "in kind" by his clients? (We can imagine game, produce and gifts arriving at Marsdon House, but this could hardly be considered adequate recompense.) How efficient was his book-keeping system? Then as now "Cash Flow" is vital for the survival and prosperity of any business. Did T.C. appreciate this? Is it likely or conceivable that he pursued clients who could not or would not pay? Was it within his nature to follow up such people diligently or even to give priority to his career over his consuming interests (particularly those of an art collector and painter)? The answers must all point in the same direction, and help to explain why he was declared insolvent in 1853, moving from the grandeur of Marston House to the more humble Hamblin House further up Cumberland Street.

The last ten years of T.C.'s life did not witness an upturn in his finances; the reverse was true and his debts steadly increased. He sold over this period many of the most prized paintings from his collection. Although there were some economies in the families lifestyle, particularly as a result of living in a smaller house, overall they conducted themselves much as before. T.C. sold and bought paintings, his work as a leading county attorney continued and he spent his recreation hours as always sketching and painting.

Impressionist style seascape 6" x 7"

Footnotes to the Woodbridge Scene

1. Crucial years in relation to his personal finances - the middle period of hie career as a lawyer and a time when his collecting continued unabated.

2. Henry Bright, 1814-1873, born at Saxmundham, apprenticed to a Woodbridge chemist in the early 1830s, reputed to have been a friend and to have painted with T.C. Certainly their style at this early period of his career was very similar.

3. Significantly, Perry Nursey was a correspondent and acquaintance of John Constable, and he could have introduced Constable to T.C. when the former was visiting Woodbridge.

4. E.F.G. is credited with coining the phrase "The Woodbridge Wits". In a letter of 1843, published in 1889, he writes "We are considered the chief Woodbridge Wits" (i.e. E.F.G., B.B. and T.C.).

5. Wallace Morfey, 'Painting the Day', page 31.

6. For the greater part of his long naval career, 'Captain' George Hailes was land-based. In fact, officially he remained a naval lieutenant, and the rank of captain was only a courtesy one.

7. At the 1832 Woodbridge auction virtually everything belonging to the Churchyards from 29 Seckford Street was sold: his extensive collection of paintings which included works by Gainsborough, Morland and John Crome, his legal and other books, household furniture and even the matrimonial bed!

8. Much of T.C.'s character is revealed in the letters of B.B. and E.F.G. B.B. writes of T.C. being "restless and craving after novelty" and "rushing hither and thither". We know from his taxing schedule as attorney, art collector and connoisseur, without being a painter in his own right, that he had great resources of both physical and mental energy.

9. T.C. exhibited at the following venues:
   1829 - Norwich
   1830 - London, Society of British Artists: 2 oils - "Cottage at Bredfield, Sussex" and "A lane at Melton, Suffolk"
   1831 - London, The Royal Academy exhibited a "Drawing from Nature" (In 1832 and 1833 the Academy failed to exhibit the landscapes T.C. submitted)
   1831 - London, Society of British Artists - 2 watercolours: "Landscape" and "Sketch from Nature"
   1832 - London, Society of British Artists - One oil and one watercolour exhibited
   1833 - London, New Society of Watercolourists
   1850 - Ipswich, Suffolk Fine Arts Committee - 16 examples of T.C.'s work exhibited: 10 oils, 6 watercolours
   1852 - Norwich

10. Miss Churchyard confirmed that T.C. rarely returned home from his daily walks in the country without two or three fresh sketches and watercolours.

Miss Churchyard, Master Charley and the Little White Mice

It is not easy to assess the effect, beneficial or adverse, of Churchyard's family on his professional and artistic career. There are few letters or documents remaining and in those available Mrs Churchyard rarely features at all. From Thomas's 1825 portrait of 'Mrs Harriet Churchyard' we can confirm her elegance and good looks, but it would seem that she had little intellectual or artistic leanings: in fact, even her role as matriarch within the family is in doubt. Some twenty years after the Churchyard marriage (and after Mrs Churchyard had given birth to at least ten children), Bernard Barton wrote to Ellen Churchyard, then a student at Mrs Jay's Bury St Edmunds Ladies' Academy: "Ma very poorly with a bad headache; muddled about her Servants and they have had Workmen about the House and Yard for ever so long, which had already kept her in didles" (old Suffolk vernacular for vexations). T.C., in one of the few existing personal documents, wrote to Emma, who was staying at Mrs Jay's academy while the rest of the family went on holiday to Aldeburgh: "Mama is certainly much better in health ... but her legs continue to trouble her, she is weak on them and they swell". This was seventeen years before her death in 1867. Certainly when T.C. died in 1865 it was Miss Ellen Churchyard as eldest daughter who played the major role in the practicalities of winding up his estate, not her mother.

T.C. died deeply in debt. This necessitated the public auction of the more important items from the Churchyard home in 1866, the Public Appeal for his family and the move from Hamblin to the smaller Penrith House. His standing within the community, where he had enjoyed deep and sincere respect, cannot be in doubt. This is substantiated by the obituaries in the local press (Appendices 2 and 3).

Mrs Churchyard 1797 - 1867 (attrib. to Harriet)

Ellen 2nd Sept 1826 - 3rd Jan 1909
This and the following five portraits are attirbuted to Harriet

Laura 3rd Feb 1830 - 12 Oct 1891

Anna 7th Feb 1832 - 19th March 1897

Elizabeth 2nd July 1834 - 8th April 1913

Catherine 14th July 1839 - 27th Nov 1889

Charles 1841 - 1929

J. Redgrave, an early T.C. portrait

The public appeal, largely orchestrated by E.F.G., confirms that neither of T.C.'s sons was able to support their mother or sisters (see Appendix [4]). Though it was not publicly known, Thomas II had been tragically widowed less than two years previously and was "wandering through the New World" as he continued to do for the remaining thirty years of his life.

E.F.G.'s assessment of the family has been much quoted over the years. It certainly reveals his reservations about them. In a letter to Marietta Nursey, widow of Perry Nursey the artist, he relates the death of Mrs Chuchyard. He comments that although it is nearly eighteen months since T.C. died, "the daughters go on as before, doing all for their house" (they were living in Penrith House, Cumberland Street, after moving from Hamblin House) "but I don't think preparing for any work ... The worst is Charley, the youngest son, who having been brought up to be idle, is not only idle but dissipated and will wring all their money out of them ... " The late George Arnott in his notes on the Churchyards describes Charley as a very spoilt boy, and says that this view of him is exemplified by the portrait of him as a young teenager, probably the work of his sister Harriet. (See illustrations at begining of chapter).

Mysteries surround Charley. We know that he was probably articled or at least worked for some years in an Ipswich lawyer's office, but the Misses Redstone thought that he also worked in an Ipswich architect's office. This would account for the fact that many of his early watercolours and oils have the quality of an architect's drawing: a good example being his very careful and precise watercolour 'Wilford Bridge' of which there are still extant at least half a dozen examples. A series of watercolours of the Seckford almshouses and dated 1871 have similar qualities.

In Country Life some time ago there was a watercolour published showing the sea-water pool and jetty at Weston-Super-Mare as a 'Mystery view by Thomas Churchyard'. Wallace Morfey notes Churchyards' works while he and his family were om holiday in the town in 1853.

Weston-Super-Mare. Note riders in both watercolours 6" x 8".

Anna Churchyard, signed A.C., inscribed Weston-Super-Mare 6" x 8"

Thomas Churchyard from the rocks below the path in previous pictures. A full power watercolour 7" x 9".

The same scene as previously, probably by Bessie. Colour notes for use upon their return to lodgings 5" x 7"

Impressionistic sea scape

Derelict cottage 6″ x 8″   A favourite study of T.C. and daughters; many similar examples to be found.

Cattle grazing in Suffolk Lane oil 12" x 10"

Doiley, attributed to Anna of 'Framlingham Castle'

Wife: (he had brought her a little present) "No William, I will not have him brought up on the bottle, look at your own nose dear!!!" (attributed to Kate)

'The Little White Mice' produced scores of Doileys 1865 -1879 (when their finances were particularly dire). Mostly pen and ink and a few examples are painted some satirical and others staight forward sketches. These they attempted to sell, often for under a 1/- (one shilling) each! 5 pence' in modern coinage.

'Dining out in a hunting neighbourhood'.
Doiley, attributed to Harriet. Fine and very detailed pen and
ink work, influenced by John Brook Hart, who had several
cartoons published by Punch in the 1870's.

Doiley, attributed to Harriet or Kate.

Ufford Church 4″ x 5¹/₂″

Martlesham Bridge
by Charley Churchyard circa 1890
8" x 11"

Wilford Bridge, Melton
by Charley Churchyard 1897
3" x 4"

From Bullards Lane, attributed to Anna

Miss Churchyard was perceived by E.F.G. as being of a different ilk from her sisters - "the little white mice" as he called them. She was a strong character, as clearly indicated in B.B.'s poem "The Young Housewife" (Appendix 5). Further, she was until a few years following T.C.'s death an accomplished and versatile artist showing at times an insight not recognised by her sisters. It should come as no surprise to find it is Ellen's hand that appears on the more important paintings bequeathed by T.C. to his daughters. The little sketch book of Woodbridge with pencil drawings dated and named 'Bessie Churchyard 1869' is again in her eldest sisters hand. Miss Churchyard was the natural leader. Her acceptance of responsibility for the family after T.C.'s death followed by that of their mother seventeen months later in 1867 confirms this. The business like approach was not appreciated by her sisters, souring their relations for several years. She had the initiative to travel to Norwich to take up a residential post, and, on returning to

woodbridge, acted as Ben Moulton's housekeeper for several years. Under the terms of Moulton's will (he died in 1883) she was left an annuity of thirty pounds for life, enabling her to live in some comfort. Her home in New Street separate her from her sisters, who continued to live at Penrith House until first Laura (1879) and later Harriet (1891) were appointed as Seckford librarians, with the old schoolmaster's house adjacent to the library as their residence. At some point around this time Charley found sanctuary with Ellen, for some twenty years sharing her New Street home or (as Major Hart expressed it) 'living off' her before in 1903 securing a place at the Seckford Almshouses. A further indication of her strength of personality was her continuing contact with E.F.G., in contrast to her sisters, who could not bear him. E.V.G. Lucas, while researching and preparing his biography "Bernard Barton and his Friends" (published 1902), visited Ellen and found her a useful, source of information.

Left: Documented as The Old Swan Inn' Southwold but in fact Cumberland House, Cumberland Street, Woodbridge. Attributed to Harriet 4$\frac{1}{2}$" x 5"

Colonel Spindlers Carriage', (the Churchyards moved from Marston House, opposite Cumberland House - 1853) attributed to Harriet 4" x 4"

Farmyard Scene with horse pond and trees, possibly at Blocks Barn, Melton   6" x 8"

Right: Reverse of above painting

The mutual dislike between E.F.G. and the remaining girls is well authenticated. The fact that he left them a bequest could be viewed as almost something of a slight, bearing in mind the size of his estate (which was in excess of £37,000, no mean figure in 1883 with no dependents), and other generous bequests to his friends. The Churchyard girls were left £100, to be divided between Laura, Anna, Harriet and Kate. It would appear that they had viewed E.F.G.'s friendship with their

'A happy new year'

The
Welcome Christmas Guest

I'm Mr Turkey, come to dine,
With your good pudding and your wine,
   As you can well suppose;
I started off in such wild haste,
For I had not much time to waste,
   So came without my clothes.

Just hide me in your larder, pray,
Be anywhere out of the way,
   I've prided like all the rest,

You'll soon see all your company,
Will with much honour welcome me,
   But not till I am dressed.

Anna.

father with distrust, probably identifying him as the main source of encouragement for their father's continual purchase of paintings during the years when increasing financial problems made this disastrous. The scandals revolving around E.F.G., which included his catastrophic marriage to Lucy Barton and his dubious relationship with Posh, caused much gossip among the Churchyard family as in the rest of sensation-loving Woodbridge. He on his part, by labelling them "the little white mice", indicated that he felt little respect for their sensitivities or their abilities. They were, however, unable to express their dislike and distrust in an overt way, dealing with it, as with all else disagreeable, by pretending it was not so: exactly like their father.

In contrast to Ellen's younger sisters, circumstantial evidence supports the fact of her strength of character. She was prepared to sell books given to her as gifts by E.F.G. and, unlike her sisters, sold paintings by her father over the years, while in her firm hand, similar to that of T.C., she confirmed the sale and authenticity of the works in writing.

Major Hart's father, John Brook Hart[2], wrote of the Churchyard girls as being "a family apart", even before the death of their parents. Not only were they, like T.C., "educated beyond their class" but, more correctly, educated beyond their means of support. There was no family wealth to provide dowries for the seven girls. The extrovert character of their father, his professional life as a leading county attorney, his friendship with the Woodbridge Wits (maybe more accurately described by Edgar Dowsing[3] as the 'Woodbridge Eccentrics'), drew attention to the family. The history of the Hailes family and the subsequent marriage of Susan and T.C. were all part of local folklore, as was the behaviour of some of the members of the extended Churchyard family.[4] The growing financial and at times personal difficulties of members of the larger family continued to focus the spotlight on them. The common characteristic of the girls, with the exception of Ellen, led them to withdraw increasingly into their own private world.

Country Child - Kate Churchyard

Cumberland Street, Woodbridge by Laura Churchyard

Cottage at Melton by Laura Churchyard

'Village children' by Harriet: late watercolour cicra 1914

Relationships were private and never to be discussed freely or openly outside the house.

Painting and sketching continued to play an active part in their lives and probably acted as an outlet or a safety valve for them all. Harriet's watercolour of Cumberland House opposite Marston House epitomises a great deal. It appears to be satirical; clearly it was painted from the privacy of Marston House. Colonel Spindler plainly is a pseudonym, while labelling the venue as "The Swan Hotel, Southwold", is yet another smokescreen to confuse any outsider who might possibly look at the painting and be able to identify not only the correct location but also the grandee depicted in the horse-drawn conveyance.

When their eldest brother Thomas (T.C.II) married Elizabeth Bardwell, almost certainly the illegimate daughter of their great uncle Isaac Churchyard (and no doubt known as such throughout the locality), no member of the Churchyard family attended the Clopton wedding, although the church is at a distance of less than five miles from Woodbridge. Three years later, when Thomas's family were drowned off the coast of Newfoundland while emigrating to start a new life in Canada, no further mention was ever made publicly of their brother or his lost family.

Charley's misdemeanours were known throughout Woodbridge and district for the greater part of his life, but his sisters, when living in No. 3 Seckford Street, never talked openly about him or appeared to notice him, despite his passing their door each time he went to the Market Hill.

The annual exchange of personal Christmas, New Year and birthday cards, individually designed and painted for each sister are very revealing. They show a warmth and humour which few outsiders could have imagined; a warmth which can be seen in many of the paintings which date from after T.C.'s death. Harriet's sketches and watercolours of children, in particular her "Village Children" which appears to have been

'Portrait' of the Churchyards family pet.

painted around 1914, shows much feeling, empathy and sympathy for the poor. The public facade was often less pleasing. Cool discipline and quietness were for instance the accepted order of the day for the Seckford library. Harriet became something of a 'grande dame', and age brought respect. No talking was allowed in the library, and any child who caused offence would be quickly ejected. Intimacy was to be shared only between the sisters and, in a very limited way, with the Redstone family throughout the long years in residence at the Old Schoolmaster's House. At the death of each sister the same peculiar ritual was carried out, first by Mrs Redstone and later by her daughter, of packing and stowing the trunks containing personal belongings in the attic. They were to remain intact until the death of the last Churchyard sister, Harriet, in 1927.

Footnotes to Miss Churchyard, Master Charley and the Little White Mice.

1. Ben Moulton, 19th century Woodbridge entrepreneur, auctioneer, and friend of T.C. His business associations in Woodbridge continued from 1830 until his death in 1885.

2. John Brook Hart, son of Daniel Hart, was a keen amateur artist like his father. He had cartoons published by Punch in the 1870s and '80s with his distinctive signature H.B.J. (being the reverse of J.B.H.). The influence of John Brook Hart can be seen in the 'Punch-like' cartoons and sketches, particularly those by Ellen, Harriet and Kate, which had a satirical element in their humour.

3. Edgar Dowsing - 1896-1984 had a lifelong love of Woodbridge and district. Born at Melton, he worked for the Notcutts, managing their Thoroughfare shop for many years. At the 1927 sale he purchased many lots for R.C. Notcutt (and some for himself) of T.C.'s paintings. Edgar Dowsing became an enthusiastic collector, and authority not only on Churchyard but the Norwich School.

4. Three major skeletons in the Churchyard cupboard which caused scandals:
    1. Benjamin Churchyard, brother of Jonathan the elder, and shoemaker at Wickham Market, brought considerable approbrium and scandal on the extended Churchyard family by fathering two bastard sons by Anne Beart; a girl nearly thirty years his junior. His eventual marriage to Anne in 1798 did not erase the stigma.
    2. Isaac Churchyard, son of Henry Churchyard, butcher of Ufford, purchased in 1807 a butcher's shop, dwelling house and slaughter house on the Market Hill, Woodbridge. Nine years later in 1816 he was widowed with two young children; surprisingly it was a further eight years before he re-married a certain Lucy Smith, a native of Great Bealings. At Isaac's death in 1833 he left not only the two children by his first marriage but a son, Henry, by his second. His finances were found to be in crisis, and T.C., as his kinsman and lawyer was in a sense doubly responsible for the surviving dependants' welfare. Over the years Mrs Lucy Churchyard's business affairs did not improve: her insolvency and eventual bankruptcy in 1848 reflected upon the standing of all the Churchyard family. From this time onwards T.C. had serious financial problems himself, leading to his own declared insolvency in 1853. It was as a result of this that he was obliged to hand over to Ben Moulton the responsibility for Lucy Chuchyard's care.
    3. T.C.'s farmer uncle Isaac (another Isaac - see Family Tree - p12) fathered a bastard daughter on one of his labourers' daughters. Isaac had taken Leah Bardwell into his home at Byng Hall, and Elizabeth their daughter was 'farmed out' locally. At seventeen Elizabeth was employed by John Woods as a domestic servant at his Cumberland Street home (John Woods was a nineteenth century Woodbridge nurseryman whose family sold their nursery to R.C. Notcutt in 1897). This was less than three hundred yards from Hamblin House, the home of T.C. and his family. The details of the ensuing romance between T.C. II and Elizabeth Bardwell are now 'lost in time'. However, this was another scandal which must have been difficult for the 'little white mice' to countenance. T.C. II's marriage to Elizabeth did not help to erase the problem or to reconcile the family.
    4. One of Charlies' favorite painting positions was to set up his easel in Seckford street, not far from Seckford library, which must have stressed the "little white mice". (See his painting of the Market Hill, see page 46).

A Prophecy Confirmed

When T.C.'s health was deteriorating in the 1860s, he began the task of dividing his most important paintings among his seven daughters. Each painting was marked precisely with the daughter's name in Ellen's clear hand. It was at this time that he made his much quoted prophecy: "My dears, there will not be any money for you when I die, but I will leave you my Paintings, which one day will be worth more than any money I could ever have hoped to have made". All his children believed implicitly that their father's work would be recognised as having a special place in the English landscape school, which helps to explain why they kept so many of his paintings. In 1927, the hoard of paintings in the care of the last surviving daughter ran into many thousands (over a thousand oils alone were sold in the subsequent auction). However, from the beginning the paintings of both T.C. and of his family had been mixed up. Many watercolours had been glued into albums, with little relation to either subject or authorship. Following the death of Harriet, Charley Churchyard, the lone surviving Churchyard and beneficiary of his late sister, with Major Hart, grandson of Daniel Hart, T.C.'s great friend and fellow amateur artist, were called in to assist in lotting the pictures for auction, and they muddled T.C.'s with his daughters' work still further.

Throughout the post-war period there has been a growing appreciation of the work of T.C., as shown by the increasing demand and the prices paid for his paintings and sketches (Appendix 6). The two biographies, of Denis Thomas and, later, Wallace Morfey, have helped to meet the need for a better understanding of his work and personality. Because of the complexities of T.C. and his family, much diligent research has been necessary to build up even a thumbnail portrait.

Throughout his life the role of his family and friends was crucial to his development as an artist. He was no loner, but a

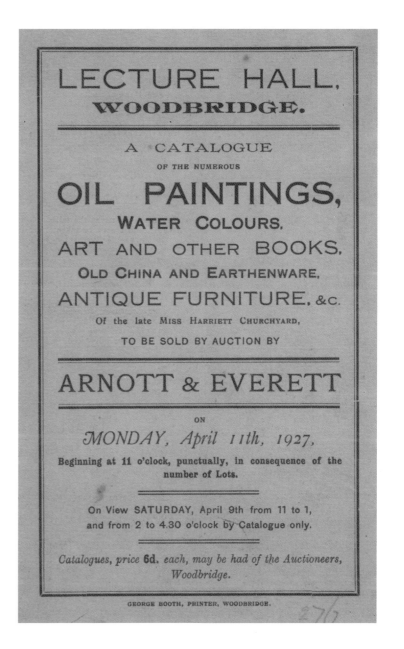

LECTURE HALL,
WOODBRIDGE.

A CATALOGUE
OF THE NUMEROUS

OIL PAINTINGS,

WATER COLOURS.

ART AND OTHER BOOKS.

OLD CHINA AND EARTHENWARE.

ANTIQUE FURNITURE, &c.

Of the late MISS HARRIETT CHURCHYARD,

TO BE SOLD BY AUCTION BY

ARNOTT & EVERETT

ON

MONDAY, April 11th, 1927,

Beginning at 11 o'clock, punctually, in consequence of the number of Lots.

On View SATURDAY, April 9th from 11 to 1, and from 2 to 4.30 o'clock by Catalogue only.

Catalogues, price **6d.** *each, may be had of the Auctioneers, Woodbridge.*

GEORGE BOOTH, PRINTER, WOODBRIDGE.

Threatening Storm 6″ x 7″

Impressionist woodland scene 6" x 7"

warm sociable person, who needed the stimulus and company of those with whom he felt comfortable working. In his last years, when he had gained confidence, often painting in his own avant-garde impressionistic style, it was his children and especially his seven daughters who jealously supported and stimulated him. None had the talent of their father, yet all, through his example and tutelage, had skills and competencies as "Churchyards" and were recognised by their contemporary amateur artists. Their work is often worthy of serious consideration, though their inability to be selective continues to obscure the merlt of both their work and that of T.C. They kept virtually every scrap of worked paper and hoard, including what might have been better discarded. This helps to explain the great variations in the quality of their paintings, the vast majority of which were personal exercises, some to be possibly developed and incorporated into later work, some simply to extend their skill, while on occasions, some were simply doodles for fun. It was the late Edgar Dowsing in conversation who voiced what many twentieth century collectors have thought for years: "When sorting out and bequeathing his most

T.C. landscape with Wickham Market Spire in background

T.C: late work

At Kyson: pencil sketch attributed to Bessie

Pen and ink sketch of Grove Farm cottage 4" x 5"
(possibly Grove Cottage, Woodbridge or
Grove Cottage, Hasketon)

Brightwell Church an early study (see p.32)

important paintings to his daughters it would have helped if Thomas had destroyed many of his lesser works". Quantity, not quality, remains one of the over-riding hazards for any Churchyard collector.

There is no simple or conclusive guide for distinguishing T.C.'s work from that of his daughters or, in some cases, that of local artists, with whom he is known to have painted. Certainly he was the guide and mentor for his children and his influence can be seen in all their work. His own hand is more confident and more decisive, and his subject treatment more masculine - his daughters often display "a softer, more feminine touch"*. As to the work of his early sketching and painting friends, notably George Rowe and Daniel Hart, it is difficult to distinguish positively by style alone which is T.C.'s work and which not, other than that both Daniel Hart and George Rowe usually

signed or monogrammed their paintings. An avenue which often helps, particularly when examining landscapes, necessitates a basic historical knowledge of the locality or some simple research. Buildings and other distinguishing man-made features can often be dated. Many years ago I was shown some fine and detailed watercolours of Melton but it became my uncomfortable duty to draw attention to the prominently visible spire of St Andrew's Church, built in 1868, three years after T.C.'s death, making it impossible for the paintings to be his work. The owners were disappointed, but their paintings themselves have quality and charm, and without this one piece of 'incriminating' evidence could easily have passed for the work of T.C.

Much of T.C.'s early work is clearly that of a copyist. The much quoted influence of Constable is more likely to have been perfected not by the few occasions when they may have sketched and painted together, but by T.C. being able carefully to examine Constable's work in his own home and by his copying, imitating and experimenting within the Constable mode of working. The Churchyard children were all instilled with the great value of copying work of the masters; even Bessie, often depicted as being the least gifted and somewhat slow, was able to reproduce her father's work accurately. This is confirmed in a dated and signed sketchbook of her work which we have photographed.

Some of the detective work which has made possible the distinguishing of his work from that of his contemporaries has been facilitated by the contribution of Thomas Churchyard enthusiasts who have often had many years' experience of

---

* Charley more often signed and dated his work (for commercial reasons), particularly his later paintings, which showed a more 'primitive' or masculine touch, and the introduction of bold figures, carts and boats (in the case of Deben or seascapes) is characteristic.

St. Andrews (New Church), Melton: Laura

THOMAS CHURCHYARD
1798 – 1865

Right: Potash cottage, Lawyer Woods Lane, Melton (a work of Charley and not as suggested by inscription on the mount - Buyer Beware!).

View from Kyson Bridge looking towards the Deben and the Tide Mill, (the railway reached Woodbridge in 1859 so we can confidently date this painting 1860 - 1865 5" x 7"

examining his work. Usually it is not one point alone but several which will lead to a general consensus. Many factors, including style, use of materials, confidence of brush-stroke and topographical details will help in the arrival at a conclusion. A friend recently put this very simply: "To be a good work by Thomas, it does not necessarily have to conform to all my preconceived ideas of technique or style, but it must excite".

It is not surprising, as T.C. was essentially an amateur and largely self-taught artist, not comprehending the techniques of both mixing and applying, that many of his paintings should have deteriorated and changed in colouring over the years. The same applies to his children's work. Many of their oils have flaked, cracked or 'bubbled', and in some instances appear to be very dark. Professional cleaning will remove surface dirt and accumulation of old varnish, but some collectors have experienced disappointment, anticipating when purchasing a dark Churchyard oil that the restorer will be able to return it more closely to how they think it originally appeared.

At the outset the canvas, cardboard or wooden board used for the painting often had insufficient preparation. Further it may have been an unsuitable medium if the board was unseasoned or had too much grain and resin. T.C. was renowned for always being in a hurry: 'rushing hither and thither', according to B.B., so it is unlikely that he would either make proper preparation or select the best medium. Added to this he was not painting to sell his work, or for posterity, but simply for self satisfaction.

Few nineteenth century artists understood how paints reacted chemically over the short term, let alone after upwards of one hundred and eighty years. It is now appreciated that oil paints often become darker. The colours change, especially if the wrong combination is applied. White and red lead-based paints commonly used in the last century are notorious for their colour instability and for their inter-reaction. Both under varnishing and later over-varnishing can similarly have a disastrous effect, and require professional restoration.

Many Churchyard watercolours (both those of T.C. and of his children) have faded and deteriorated. The contemporary gentle sepia effect found in many of his watercolours is far removed from what originally would often have been a bright or even colourful work. This may be observed if the old mount is carefully 'eased' away and perhaps a small part which has been covered can be seen in its original brightness. Sunlight, while often being blamed for causing the most damage, is not the only factor; and fading also may result in a change of pigment colouring over the years. For instance, in many of Charley's watercolours the greens now appear distinctly blue, while the blue of the sky has an unnatural hue. 'Foxing', caused by the damp atmosphere and fabric of many traditional Suffolk country houses, has also blighted many nineteenth century watercolours. This condition can be treated by the professional restorer - at a cost! Non-acid-free paper is also evident both in that used for the watercolour itself and for the mounting card or paper. In the case of the latter modern mounting card is the solution: on occasion where the old mount has marked the watercolour a small loss around the watercolour is a justifiable sacrifice.

All the foregoing factors must be carefully taken into account when purchasing Churchyard paintings - especially as prices continue to rise at an alarming rate. Let the buyer beware!

Examples of T.C.'s work are now to be found hanging in the major British and many international galleries (Appendix 6), fulfilling his prophecy of so many years ago. The time it has taken would no doubt have surprised both Thomas Churchyard and his children.

Above: Study of Cistus, oil on panel. A good exa,mple of 'darkening' over the years as a result of chemical reaction of paint mixtures.

Left: Jetty Lane now the Avenue, Woodbridge by Charley cicra 1880

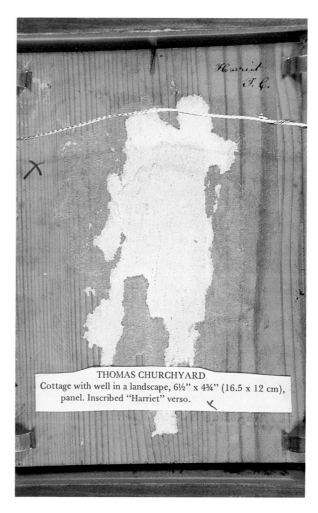

THOMAS CHURCHYARD
Cottage with well in a landscape, 6½" x 4¾" (16.5 x 12 cm),
panel. Inscribed "Harriet" verso.

Caption on reverse of oil

Appendix 1

To T.C. - At forty-one (1839)

On the birthday of a King,
Or a Queen, let Laureates sing;
And to recompense their lay,
Quaff their sack, or pouch their pay;
In such odes I see no fun;
Here's to Tom - at forty-one!

If a Poet's wish could tell,
Doubt not I would wish thee well;
Yet what could best wish of mine
Give - but is already thine?
Wife and bairns, surpassed by none -
These are thine at forty-one!

With a good house o'er thy head,
And a table - amply spread;
With a fire-side warm and bright,
Faces all in smiles bedight;
Thus may Life's sands sparkling run
As they do at forty-one.

With good paintings on each well,
Holding sense and sight in thrall;
Morlands, Constables and Cromes -
Good as grace much prouder domes,
Sip thy wine and bite thy bun,
And so welcome forty-one!

With good pictures of thy own,
Wearing Nature's tint and tone;
And a love for others, too,
Be they but to Nature true.
What with brush, and dog and gun,
Thou'st still young at forty-one!

May old age forbear to mar
E'en a puff of thy cigar,
Or impair thine eye or hand,
Or o'ercloud thy household band;
But may every boon be thine
Friendship's blessing would assign.
Now my Birthday rhyme is done
Good-bye! Tom! at forty-one!

> Bernard Barton, 1839.
> Special composition for T.C.'s Forty-First Birthday

Appendix 2

The following Notice of the deceased appeared under the head of the Woodbridge News ln the "Ipswich Journal" of August 25, 1865.

"DEATH OF THOMAS CHURCHYARD, Esq - It is our melancholy duty this week to announce to our readers the death of our talented townsman, Thomas Churchyard, Esq. Brought up from his early youth to the study of the law, and with a brilliant intellect, there is no doubt, if his heart had been in his profession, he would have grasped its highest honours. Very many of our readers yet hear ringing in their ears his clear and nervously eloquent delivery of some legal distinction; an eloquence that not only enchanted all his hearers, but often lent a positive grace to the dry details of many an uninteresting case. His addresses, whether to the Bench or the Jury, were distinguished by a refined and dignified courtesy, so that whatever he advanced always commanded at once the attention and respect of his audience. Many a luckless wight has had cause to thank him for hair breadth escapes from the penalties of the law; his thorough knowledge of the intricacies of his profession enabling him often to convert defeat into victory, and turn the trembling scale in favour of his clients. United to this, his manner was polished and gentlemanly in the extreme; his conversation full of wit and his company at all times amusing and delightful. His devotion to the fine arts was to him the very "breath of life"; and it may be questioned whether there is now living a finer judge of the Early English Landcape School than he was. Old Crome, Wilson, Gainsborough, Morland - in these more particularly; but above all and before all, in Old Crome he revelled and delighted. Indeed, he might almost be said to be the man who first brought Crome's pictures into the high estimation they are now held; at all events, he was the first who ever ventured on a "long price" for his works. Those who knew him best can yet picture the delight with which he introduced them to some new acquisition, or mayhap an old acquaintance, parted with or exchanged years ago, welcomed back to his collection like a lost sheep returned to the fold. He himself was an artist of the highest excellence, and his works almost invariably show his affectionate reverence for the great masters we have named. Crome he studied and copied with such faithful exactitude as (on more than one occasion) to deceive the most eminent connoisseursl An ardent lover of nature, he might daily be seen sketching some favourite spot; and his pictures are conspicuous for their fidelity and truthfulness. Botany, also, was a favourite pursuit, and in his early time he made numerous drawings for a work on that subject of some note. He died quite suddenly on Saturday morning early, in his 67th year; disease of the heart, accelerated by some pressing anxiety, the immediate cause. He was devotedly attached to his family, and his well-known form, attended by some of them, will be missed in our daily haunts for many a long day. His remains, followed by a few chosen friends and members of his professlon, were quietly and unostentatiously interred at Melton on Wednesday."

Appendix 3

From the "Suffolk Chronicle", Saturday, September 23, 1865.
WOODBRIDGE COUNTY COURT, MONDAY, September 18.
(Before J. Worlledge, Esq., Judge)

THE LATE MR. CHURCHYARD

His Honour, on entering the Court, said: "In taking my seat on this occasion, I cannot but refer to a melancholy loss which this Court and this town have sustained since I last was here. I had the pleasure of knowing the late Mr. Churchyard for many years, both privately and in his public capacity. In his private capacity I ever appreciated his refined mind, his genial spirit, and his courteous manner, but it was chiefly as an advocate in this Court that I value him; for while on one hand he did his duty fearlessly and ably to his clients, he never tried to mislead me or to overreach his opponents by unworthy arts; and he never wasted the public time by keeping up useless discussions. By such conduct he won my sincere respect and entire confidence, and in thus alluding to him I beg briefly to express my opinion that in him I have lost a most valuable aid in the discharge of my duty to the public in the administration of justice, and I beg leave thus publicly to express my tribute to his memory and my sincere sympathy with his family in their severe affliction, and understanding that his affairs are not left exactly in that position in which it was desirable, I shall be happy according to my means to contribute to the support of his family."

Appendix 4

THE LATE THOMAS CHURCHYARD, ESQ.

Your sympathy is most earnestly solicited on behalf of the family of the late Mr THOMAS CHURCHYARD, Solicitor, Woodbridge, who died very suddenly on the l9th August last, leaving a Widow and seven Daughters totally unprovided for: his two Sons not being in a position to give them the smallest assistance.

Mr CHURCHYARD was well known throughout the County of Suffolk, and was much and deservedly esteemed by his professional brethren.

It is earnestly hoped that this appeal will be so met as to offer to the Widow and Daughters the double solace of respect to his memory, and a provision for those he so dearly loved.

The following Sums in aid of a fund for the support of the widow and the advancement in life of the daughters have already been promised, and any donation you may be pleased to send will be applied to the same purpose.

A Provisional Committee has been formed for carrying this into effect, and your early reply will be deemed a favour by

         Your most obedient Servant,
         J. LODER,
         Hon. Sec. pro. tem.

	£. 8. d.
J. Purcell Fitz-Gerald, Esq, J.P.	100. O. O.
E. Fitz-Gerald, Esq.	100. O. O.
Sir Fitz-Roy Kelly, M.P.	50. O. O.
Sir W.P. Wood, Vice Chancellor	50. O. O.
Charles Austin, Esq., Q.C. and Chairman of Quarter Sessions	25. O. O.
Rolls Rouse, Esq., Barrister at Law	25. O. O.
Benjamin Moulton, Esq.	25. O. O.
Geo. Mooe, Esq., Solicitor	25. O. O.
Lofty, Potter & Son, Solicitors, London	25. O. O.
J.R. Wood, Esq., Solicitor	20. O. O.
J. Worlledge, Esq., Judge of County Court	15. O. O.
R.A. Reeve, Esq., Solicitor	15. O. O.

	£. 8. d.
J.W. Rouse, Esq., Solicitor	10. O. O.
Foster, Burroughs, & Robberds, Solicitors, Norwich	5. O. O.
Richard Bohun, Esq., Solicitor, Beccles	5. O. O.
W. Hartcup, Solicitor, Bungay	5. 5. O.
Robin J. Pollard, Solicitor, Ipswich	5. O. O.
H.W. Garrod, Solicitor, Diss	5. O. O.
Dalton & Hill, Solicitors, Ipswich	2. 2. O.
H.K. Moseley, Esq., Solicitor, Framlingham	2. 2. O.
Keith & Co, Solicitors, Norwich	2. 2. O.
W. Willins, Esq., Solicitor, Norwich	1. 1. O.
C.E. Tuck, Esq., Norwich	1. 1, O,
Jay & Pilgrim, Solicltors, Norwich	1. 1. O.

Donations will be received by Mr Loder; at Messrs. Alexanders; or Messrs. Bacon, Cobbold & Co, Bankers, Woodbridge.
(Note the apparent absense of small donations from local personages. Does this indicate that the Churchyard family were not popular in Woodbridge?)

Appendix 5

To a Very Young House-wife

To write a book of Household Song,
  Without one verse to thee,
Whom I have known and loved so long,
  Were all unworthy me.

Have I not seen thy needle plied
  With as much ready glee,
As if it were thy greatest pride
  A sempstress famed to be?

Have I not ate pies, puddings, tarts,
  And bread - thy hand had kneaded,
All excellent - as if those arts
  Here all that thou hadst heeded.

Have I not seen thy cheerful smile,
  And heard thy voice - as gay,
As if such household cares, the while,
  To thee were sport and play?

Yet can thy pencil copy well
  Landscape, or flower, or face;
And thou canst waken music's spell
  With simple, natural grace.
Thus variously to play thy part,
  Before thy teens are spent,
Honours far more thy head, and heart,
  Than mere accomplishment!

So wear the wreath thou well hast won;
  And be it understood
I frame it not in idle fun
  For girlish womanhood.

But in it may a lesson lurk,
  Worth teaching now-a-days;
That girls may do all household work,
  Nor lose a poet's praise!

Taken from Bernard Barton's Book of Household Verses
Published 1845.

Appendix 6

Letter from Wallace Morfey to George Arnott with reference to
purchase of Churchyard oil by the Tate in 1977

Suffolk Scene - oil 10" x 12"

Fine oil of woodland scene with donkey cart,
left to Emma by her father
(insription on reverse)   24″ x 20″

Autumn at Christchurch near Oxford

Woodbridge Quay

Bibliography

Arnott George	Suffolk Estuary 1950
Beckett R.B	John Constable's Correspondence 1967
Bennett Chloe	The Norwich School 1977
Day Harold	Suffolk School Painters 1971 - Days Diary 1972
Morfey Wallace	Painting the Day - Thomas Churchyard of Woodbridge - Boydell Press 1986
Thomas Denis	Thomas Churchyard of Woodbridge 1967
Wright Thomas	The Life of Edward Fitzgerald 1904
White William	Suffolk Directory 1844 & 1855

The Author

Robert Blake's family have lived in the Woodbridge area for many generations. As a child he moved to Melton immediately after the Second World War and his father was the village blacksmith until his death in 1993.

For many years Robert was an antique dealer both at Melton and Saxmundham. In recent years he has pursued a more academic career, having gained honours degrees and a University diploma.

Robert now manages the family firm at Melton and carries on his own business and academic interests both in Suffolk and Yorkshire. He writes on a wide variation of subjects ranging from social and historical fields; in addition he and his wife have a great interest in all matters relating to the local community.